Intermediate Guide to Designing NFTs.

A practical approach for Programmers

By

Prof. Stephen W. Bradeley BSC (Hons)

Intermediate Guide to Designing NFTs

COPYRIGHT

ABOUT ME

Writer profile

My name is Steve Bradeley and I am 66 years old (2022). I studied Exercise and Health at Staffordshire University between 1993 and 1996. I earned a science degree with honours and have since written 116 ebooks and over 20 paperback and hardcover books. I spent over 15 years as working as a private personal trainer working with clients will a full array of medical conditions. I also set up the Exercise on Prescription Scheme in the Staffordshire Moorlands in the United Kingdom. Which is still running successfully today.

For the last 15 years I have been helping students to learn English and pass the IELTS examination. I program as a hobby and am self taught.

CONTENTS

Table of Contents

BOOK OUTLINE

Book Outline: Advanced Guide to Designing and Writing NFTs. You will be able to find this new book on Amazon within the next few months. You can also find my previous book on NFTs here

BOOK ONE: **https://www.amazon.com/dp/B0C9S84Z5J**

BOOK THREE: **https://www.amazon.com/dp/B0B3RNYYRX**

I. Introduction

   A. The importance of NFTs in the digital art world

   B. The evolving applications of NFTs

II. Prerequisites

   A. Familiarity with blockchain technology

   B. Programming knowledge

     1. Solidity language

     2. Smart contracts

   C. Creativity and design skills

III. Designing NFTs

   A. Conceptualizing your NFT project

     1. Identifying a niche or target market

     2. Creating a unique value proposition

B. Creating digital art assets

    1. Design principles for NFTs

    2. File formats best suited for NFTs

IV. Writing the code for NFTs

  A. Overview of Ethereum blockchain and smart contracts

  B. Solidity syntax and features for NFT development

    1. ERC-721 standard for non-fungible tokens

    2. ERC-1155 standard for multiple token types

  C. Developing a custom smart contract for your NFT project

V. Testing and deploying your NFT smart contract on the Ethereum network

  A. Local testing using Truffle and Ganache

  B. Deploying on public testnets (Ropsten, Rinkeby, etc.)

  C. Deploying to the Ethereum Mainnet

VI. Uploading and selling your NFTs on marketplaces

  A. Overview of popular NFT marketplaces (OpenSea, Rarible, etc.)

  B.Signing up and setting up an account on a marketplace (wallet linking)

Intermediate Guide to Designing NFTs

C.Formatting your digital art for upload (Metadata standards)

D.Establishing ownership of your digital assets (Token mapping)

E.Pricing and token economics

F.Promoting your NFT

VII. Advanced topics

A. Cross-chain development and interoperability

1. Using bridges between networks

2. Developing NFTs for multiple blockchain platforms

B. NFT royalties and secondary sales

C. NFT gaming and virtual worlds

VIII. Case studies and success stories

A. Notable NFT projects, artists, and creators

B. Lessons learned from successful NFT launches

IX. Conclusion and future outlook

A. Potential uses of NFTs beyond digital art and collectibles

B. Predictions for the evolution of the NFT market and technology

Introduction

The importance of NFTs in the digital art world

In the 21st century, the digital art world has been revolutionized by the introduction of Non-Fungible Tokens (NFTs). These unique, blockchain-based assets have opened up new possibilities for artists, collectors, and investors alike, transforming the way we perceive and interact with digital art. In this book, we will explore the importance of NFTs in today's digital art landscape and how they are reshaping the future of creative expression.

A New Era of Ownership and Value

Before the emergence of NFTs, digital art faced significant challenges in terms of ownership and valuation. Digital files could be easily copied and shared, making it difficult for artists to profit from their work or for collectors to establish a sense of ownership. NFTs have changed this by providing a secure method of authenticating and verifying ownership through blockchain technology. Each NFT is unique and cannot be replicated or replaced, ensuring that collectors have a one-of-a-kind piece of art.

Breaking Down Barriers for Artists

NFTs have opened up new avenues for artists to showcase their work and monetize their creations. By issuing an NFT, artists can now sell their art directly to collectors worldwide without relying on traditional galleries or auction houses. This democratization allows emerging and niche artists to reach a broader audience while retaining more control over their work. The potential for direct communication between artists and collectors also fosters stronger connections and provides valuable feedback for future creations.

Creating New Investment Opportunities

The growing popularity of NFTs has led to increased financial opportunities in the digital art world. As these tokens prove their worth as both valuable collectible items and lucrative investment assets, more people are becoming interested in participating in this burgeoning market. Additionally, creative industries like music, film, literature, and even virtual real estate are also adopting NFT technology—generating further excitement around the potential for growth.

Promoting Sustainability

Another essential aspect of NFTs is the potential to promote sustainability in the art world. With digital art, there are no physical materials involved—eliminating waste from production, shipping, and storage. Blockchain technology also allows for transparent tracking of each artwork's provenance, reducing the risk of fraud and counterfeit items entering the market. Through these benefits, NFTs are paving the way for a more environmentally friendly and ethical art industry.

In conclusion, the rise of Non-Fungible Tokens has heralded a new era in the digital art world—one that breaks down barriers for creators and collectors while providing unique investment opportunities. As we continue to witness its growing impact, it is clear that NFTs have established themselves as an essential force in reshaping the creative landscape of the 21st century.

The Evolving Applications of NFTs: Unlocking New Possibilities in the Digital World

Non-fungible tokens (NFTs) have taken the world by storm, evolving from a niche concept within the world of cryptocurrencies to a mainstream phenomenon in just a matter of months. But what makes NFTs such a hot topic, and how are they changing the way we interact with digital assets?

Intermediate Guide to Designing NFTs

In this, book we are going to explore the evolving applications of NFTs and how they are unlocking new possibilities in various industries.

Understanding NFTs

To fully appreciate the impact of NFTs, it's essential to know what they are and how they work. Unlike cryptocurrencies such as Bitcoin or Ethereum, which are fungible and can be exchanged for one another, non-fungible tokens represent unique digital assets that cannot be replicated or replaced. This uniqueness is verified via blockchain technology, ensuring the authenticity and ownership of each NFT.

Revolutionizing Digital Art & Collectibles

One of the primary ways in which NFTs have caught the public's attention is through their use in digital art and collectables. Artists now have the ability to create limited-edition digital artworks that can be bought, sold, and traded just like physical pieces. This not only provides a new avenue for artists to monetize their work but also allows collectors to own and showcase rare digital assets.

NFTs in Gaming and Virtual Worlds

Another exciting development in the world of NFTs is their integration into gaming and virtual worlds. Characters, skins, items, and even virtual land can all be represented as NFTs, allowing users to own them truly. This opens up entirely new possibilities for users to trade and invest in digital objects with tangible value across different gaming platforms or virtual worlds.

Tokenization of Physical Assets

NFTs also hold tremendous potential for tokenizing real-world assets such as property, artwork, cars, watches, or any other valuable item. By turning these assets into unique digital tokens, individuals can trade, sell, or even offer fractional ownership of these physical items. This not only makes investing in high-value assets more accessible to a wider audience but can also increase the liquidity and efficiency of asset markets.

The Future of NFTs

While we've already witnessed several emerging use cases for NFTs, there's no doubt that we're only scratching the surface of their potential applications. As the technology continues to mature and gain widespread adoption, there are countless opportunities for integration with different industries and platforms. From digital identity management to decentralized finance and beyond, the future of non-fungible tokens is promising and full of exciting possibilities.

In conclusion, the evolving applications of NFTs demonstrate their transformational potential in revolutionizing how we interact with digital and physical assets alike. As more industries embrace this technology, we can expect to see an even greater impact on our digital lives, unlocking new economic opportunities and reshaping the way we think about ownership in the 21st century.

Prerequisites

Familiarity with blockchain technology

The Art and Science of Designing NFTs: Essential Prerequisites and Familiarity with Blockchain Technology

In recent years, non-fungible tokens (NFTs) have taken the digital art world by storm, offering creators a unique way to monetize their work and collectors an exciting new avenue for investment. Designing NFTs may appear simple at first glance, but it requires a careful balancing act between creativity and understanding the underlying technology – blockchain.

Intermediate Guide to Designing NFTs

So, what are the prerequisites for designing NFTs and how to develop a familiarity with blockchain technology?

1. Grasping the concept of non-fungibility

Before diving into designing NFTs, it's crucial to understand what sets non-fungible tokens apart from their fungible counterparts. While fungible tokens (such as cryptocurrencies like Bitcoin) are interchangeable, non-fungible tokens represent distinct digital assets. Each NFT has a unique identifier, ensuring its ownership and provenance can be easily verified on the blockchain.

2. Understanding blockchain technology

Blockchain is a decentralized and distributed ledger system that stores information across multiple computer networks instead of a centralized database. Each block in the chain contains transaction data and is secured by cryptography. Familiarizing yourself with how blockchain functions is vital for creating NFTs because these unique tokens exist on this very platform.

3. Choosing the right platform

There are multiple platforms where you can create, buy, and sell NFTs, such as Ethereum, Binance Smart Chain, and Flow. Each has its benefits and drawbacks in terms of transaction fees, ease of use, and environmental impact. Research each platform carefully before launching your NFT project.

4. Developing your art or digital asset

An important aspect of designing NFTs is creating distinctive digital art or assets that will intrigue potential buyers—be it artwork, music files, virtual collectibles, or even domain names. Take the time to develop your skills in various digital art tools and platforms, ensuring your creations stand out in a busy marketplace.

5. Learning smart contract basics

A smart contract is a self-executing contract that contains the terms of an agreement directly in code. Understanding how smart contracts work is vital for designing NFTs, as they control the process of minting (creating) and transferring token ownership. Some platforms offer pre-built templates for NFT creation, while others require you to write custom code.

6. Minting your NFT

Once you've designed your digital asset and have a grasp on blockchain technology and smart contracts, it's time to mint your NFT. The process involves uploading your creation to an NFT marketplace and specifying details such as pricing, royalties, and other metadata that will be associated with the token.

7. Marketing your NFT

Designing an exceptional NFT is only half the battle—you must market it effectively if you want it to sell. Utilize social media channels, create eye-catching content, and engage with online communities to raise awareness of your unique digital creation.

In conclusion, designing NFTs goes beyond merely creating captivating digital assets; it involves developing a foundational understanding of blockchain technology and its nuances. By taking the time to learn about non-fungibility, blockchain platforms, smart contracts, and effective marketing strategies, you'll set yourself up for success in the rapidly expanding world of non-fungible tokens.

As the world of digital art and cryptocurrencies continue to intersect, artists and designers are turning their attention to the rapidly growing world of non-fungible tokens (NFTs). Among the key factors in creating impressive and valuable NFTs is having a solid understanding of programming. This section will explore the importance of programming knowledge when designing NFTs and how it can take your digital creations to new heights.

Understanding Smart Contracts

One of the foundational elements of NFTs is the use of smart contracts. These self-executing contracts are built upon blockchain technology, primarily Ethereum, and include specific instructions and terms that define the NFT's attributes and functionalities. Being well-versed in programming languages such as Solidity or JavaScript will enable you to create sophisticated smart contracts that help your NFTs stand out from the rest.

Customizing NFT Attributes

As a designer, you want your work to be original, unique, and capable of capturing your audience's imagination. By delving into programming, you can create customized attributes for your NFTs that set them apart from the rest. From incorporating dynamic visual elements to adding interactive features, understanding code opens up limitless possibilities for artistic innovation and expression.

Intermediate Guide to Designing NFTs

Interoperability Across Platforms

An essential aspect of designing NFTs is ensuring their compatibility and accessibility across various platforms, including digital marketplaces, galleries, games, or virtual reality environments. With programming knowledge under your belt, you'll be better equipped to understand the specific technical requirements for different platforms and ensure your NFT designs can seamlessly integrate without any issues.

Improved Security Measures

With high demand comes potential security risks. As NFTs gain more traction in the digital space, instances of fraud, theft, and counterfeiting have emerged. Having a strong foundation in programming can help you incorporate security measures into your designs and smart contracts, protecting both your work and potential buyers from bad actors in the space.

Efficient Collaboration

As the NFT ecosystem continues to grow, opportunities to collaborate with other artists, developers, and collectors are bound to increase. Possessing programming knowledge makes it easier for you to communicate with fellow creators and engineers, facilitating smooth collaboration and helping you bring your ideas to life more effectively.

In conclusion, mastering programming skills when designing NFTs can help you create unique digital art pieces while ensuring they are secure and seamlessly integrate across multiple platforms. As the NFT market continues to evolve, staying ahead of the curve by possessing this crucial skill will undoubtedly enhance your creative potential and give your work a competitive edge.

Let's dive into the world of programming languages used in the creation, management, and trading of these digital masterpieces.

1. Solidity: The Backbone of NFTs

As the primary language used for writing Ethereum-based smart contracts, Solidity is arguably the most crucial programming language to learn when it comes to NFT design. Most NFTs are created using Ethereum's ERC-721 or ERC-1155 token standards, which require developers to have a strong grasp of Solidity. This language allows you to define the rules and behavior of your NFT, such as ownership, metadata, and transferability.

2. JavaScript: A Versatile Language

When creating an interactive user interface (UI) for showcasing or trading NFTs on a website, JavaScript is a go-to language. It can be used in combination with other languages like HTML and CSS to create visually appealing and functional websites or applications. Additionally, JavaScript works well with web3.js - a library that facilitates interaction with Ethereum-based smart contracts from within web applications.

3. Python: Rapid Prototyping and Powerful Libraries

Python is another popular choice for working with blockchain technology and creating NFTs due to its readability, adaptability, and extensive library support. Libraries like Web3.py allow developers to interact with Ethereum smart contracts using Python. Moreover, it's an excellent option for developers who prefer focusing on rapid prototyping without getting bogged down in complex syntax.

4. IPFS: Not a Language but Essential Tooling

While not a programming language itself, IPFS (InterPlanetary File System) is an essential tool in the NFT space. NFTs typically consist of token data on a blockchain and the actual content (art, music, etc.) stored separately. IPFS serves as a decentralized storage solution, ensuring that the digital content associated with NFTs remains accessible and resistant to censorship.

In conclusion, designing NFTs involves a combination of programming languages and tools to create unique, valuable, and engaging digital assets. Solidity serves as the foundational language for developing the smart contract component of your NFTs. Simultaneously, JavaScript and Python provide web development capabilities and interaction with smart contracts. Lastly, don't forget about IPFS for secure, decentralized storage of your digital art and content. By mastering these languages and tools, you'll be well on your way to creating compelling NFT projects that captivate audiences worldwide.

Solidity language

A crucial component of creating these unique digital assets is the Solidity programming language. In this section, we'll explore the foundation of Solidity and provide examples to help you become familiar with its use in designing NFTs.

A Brief Introduction to Solidity

Solidity is a high-level, contract-oriented programming language primarily used for designing smart contracts on blockchain platforms like

Ethereum. The language shares similarities with JavaScript and C++, making it relatively easy for developers familiar with these languages to learn. The appeal of Solidity lies in its ability to facilitate the creation of decentralized applications (dApps), NFTs, and other blockchain-based products.

Examples of Solidity in Designing NFTs

1. Creating an ERC-721 Token:

ERC-721 is the most widely used token standard for creating NFTs on the Ethereum blockchain. To begin, you'd need to import the OpenZeppelin library – a collection of secure and tested smart contracts:

```solidity
pragma solidity ^0.8.0;

import "@openzeppelin/contracts/token/ERC721/ERC721.sol";

contract MyNFT is ERC721 {
   constructor() ERC721("MyNFT", "MNFT") {}
}
```

In this example, we're creating a simple ERC-721 token named "MyNFT" with a symbol of "MNFT". It's an elementary example that demonstrates how to use Solidity to create an NFT.

2. Implementing a Minting Function:

Once you've set up your basic ERC-721 token, you can implement a minting function to create new NFTs:

```solidity
pragma solidity ^0.8.0;


import "@openzeppelin/contracts/token/ERC721/ERC721.sol";

import "@openzeppelin/contracts/utils/Counters.sol";


contract MyNFT is ERC721 {

    using Counters for Counters.Counter;

    Counters.Counter private _tokenIds;


    constructor() ERC721("MyNFT", "MNFT") {}


    function mintNFT(address recipient, string memory tokenURI) public returns (uint256) {
```

```
    _tokenIds.increment();


    uint256 newItemId = _tokenIds.current();

    _mint(recipient, newItemId);

    _setTokenURI(newItemId, tokenURI);


    return newItemId;

  }

}
```
```

This mintNFT function allows you to mint a new NFT with a specific Token ID and assign it to the desired recipient's address. The tokenURI parameter serves as a unique identifier pointing to the NFT's metadata.

These examples showcase the Solidity language's capabilities in designing NFTs. As you explore further and grasp more advanced concepts, you'll be able to create increasingly complex and feature-rich NFTs.

In conclusion, the Solidity language is a vital tool for developers looking to enter the world of NFTs. By understanding its fundamental constructs and reviewing practical examples, you can pave your way to success in
```

the burgeoning realm of digital assets.

Smart Contracts

Demystifying Smart Contracts: A Comprehensive Guide and Solidity Coding Example

One innovative concept that has emerged as a key player is the smart contract. In simple terms, a smart contract is a self-executing digital agreement between two or more parties, with the terms of the agreement being written directly into lines of code. Operating on a decentralized platform like Ethereum, these contracts have the potential to revolutionize industries ranging from finance to supply chain management, by enhancing trust and security while minimizing intermediaries and costs.

What Is a Smart Contract?

A smart contract can be thought of as programmable logic that automatically executes once predefined conditions are met. The underlying concept is not new – the idea for such digital contracts was first introduced in 1994 by American computer scientist Nick Szabo. However, it was only with the rise of blockchain technology that they started gaining widespread attention and adoption.

Smart contracts are mainly associated with Ethereum – a decentralized platform that supports custom tokens (ERC20) and decentralized applications (DApps). But it's important to note that they also exist on other blockchains like NEO and EOS.

Coding Example: Solidity Language

To better understand how smart contracts work, let's dive into an example created using Solidity - a programming language specifically designed for writing smart contracts on the Ethereum blockchain.

Suppose we have two individuals, Alice and Bob, who want to bet on the outcome of a coin flip. Rather than relying on traditional intermediaries or complex legal agreements, they decide to use a smart contract that automatically pays out to the winner based on the result.

A simple version of their smart contract in Solidity might look like this:

```solidity
pragma solidity ^0.6.0;

contract CoinFlipBet {
    address payable public alice;
```

```solidity
address payable public bob;

bool public aliceChoice;

uint256 public betAmount;

enum State { Created, Locked, Inactive }

State public state;


constructor(bool _aliceChoice) public payable {

    alice = msg.sender;

    aliceChoice = _aliceChoice;

    betAmount = msg.value;

    state = State.Created;

}


function acceptBet(bool _bobChoice) public payable {

    require(msg.value == betAmount);

    bob = msg.sender;

    state = State.Locked;


    bool result = (block.timestamp % 2 == 0);

    if (aliceChoice == result) {

        alice.transfer(address(this).balance);
```

```
    } else {

        bob.transfer(address(this).balance);

    }


        state = State.Inactive;

    }

}
```
```

This basic example demonstrates the core functionalities of a smart contract and how it can execute an agreement between two parties without any need for external enforcement or intermediaries. Real-world scenarios would involve more complex logic, but the underlying principle remains the same – utilizing blockchain technology to create trustless, secure, and efficient digital agreements.

As we move forward into the era of digitalization, smart contracts will undoubtedly play an increasingly pivotal role in shaping a diverse range of industries. By promoting decentralization, transparency, and automation, these digital agreements promise greater efficiency and trust in a multitude of sectors - from finance and real estate to medical records and voting systems. The potential for growth is immense, making smart contracts a fascinating topic to explore and understand.
```

As this market expands, the demand for creativity and design skills in NFT creation is skyrocketing. This paragraph will explore the essential design elements and creative approaches needed when crafting NFTs that truly stand out in the ever-competitive digital landscape.

Understand Your Audience

The first step in creating a compelling NFT is to understand your target audience. Research current trends within your niche to determine what designs appeal to potential buyers. Look for patterns or themes that resonate with collectors and fans, as this can guide you in the development of your NFT concept.

Conceptualize Your Design

A solid concept forms the backbone of any successful NFT creation. Aim to create a story or idea that captivates the viewer's imagination. As you start designing, consider key elements like color schemes, typography, illustrations, and animations that not only align with your chosen storyline but also distinguish your work from others in the marketplace.

Compose a Cohesive Narrative

While visual elements are crucial, they are only half of what makes an NFT successful. A cohesive narrative helps create immersive experiences for viewers — be it through storytelling prompts embedded within an artwork or a series of connected pieces that form a broader creative vision. Explore ways to integrate text and invent lore for characters or environments in order to foster both emotional connection and intellectual investment in your NFT project.

Embrace Experimentation

One of the defining characteristics of NFT art is its inherent adaptability. Unlike traditional art forms, digital NFTs allow creators to push boundaries with innovative techniques like motion graphics, 3D rendering, virtual exhibitions, and augmented reality. Embracing experimentation enables you to produce groundbreaking work that captures attention even within a saturated market.

Stay Current and Adapt

As the NFT landscape continually evolves, staying updated on new tools, platforms, and trends is essential. By staying informed, you can adjust your creative approach and harness new opportunities to showcase your work. Never be afraid to reinvent yourself or pivot based on trends and technological changes.

Leverage Social Media

A strong online presence is integral to linking with fellow creators, collectors, and fans in the NFT community. Actively engage by asking for feedback, sharing work in progress, and participating in social media discussions. This will not only deepen your understanding of the market but also assist in attracting potential buyers interested in your unique creative vision.

In conclusion, standing out in the saturated NFT market requires a blend of exceptional design skills, authentic storytelling prowess, an innovative mindset, and the ability to connect with potential buyers. As you embark on your NFT journey, embrace these practices to create captivating artwork that speaks to the changing times and leaves a lasting impact on digital art enthusiasts.

Designing NFTs

Conceptualizing your NFT project

Designing and conceptualizing NFTs: Bringing your digital art to life

The world of Non-Fungible Tokens (NFTs) is taking the digital art scene by storm. As more artists and collectors are drawn to this innovative form of digital ownership, learning how to create and conceptualize your own NFT project is an invaluable skill.

1. Find your niche and develop your concept

Before you start designing your NFTs, it's essential to have a clear concept of what you want to create. To stand out in the competitive NFT space, focus on finding your unique niche. Research popular themes in the market, but don't be afraid to delve into unexplored subjects that showcase your artistic style. Once you've honed in on a theme or subject, begin brainstorming cohesive concepts and ideas for your NFT series or collection.

2. Master your artistic tools

Creating high-quality digital art requires skill and a good understanding of design software like Adobe Creative Suite or industry-geared programs like Procreate, Blender, or Cinema 4D. If you're new to designing digitally, consider taking online courses or receiving mentorship from experienced digital artists to maximize the potential of these tools.

3. Focus on quality and originality

Quality is key when it comes to designing NFTs. High-resolution files ensure that your art looks professional on various screens and devices. Additionally, strive for originality in your designs; remember that plagiarism or copying other artists' work can lead to serious consequences in the thriving NFT community.

4. Incorporate metadata and attributes

NFTs are more than just visual artwork; they also contain metadata—information about the piece embedded directly into the token itself. This might include descriptions, rarity rankings, or unique attributes, which can add value and depth to your NFT. By incorporating this information, you'll not only give interested parties a better understanding of your work but also improve your NFT's discoverability on platforms where they might be sold.

5. Prepare for minting and launching

Once your designs and metadata are ready, it's time to start thinking about the "minting" process—converting your digital assets into tokens on a blockchain. Research different blockchain platforms (e.g., Ethereum, Binance Smart Chain) and choose one that aligns with your goals and preferences in terms of fees and environmental impact.

You should also decide on the scope of your launch—will you be releasing a single piece or an entire collection? Plan out how you will promote your NFTs, using social media channels or teaming up with influencers in the field to create buzz around your art.

6. Engage with the community

Last but not least, remember that the NFT market is a social ecosystem built on interactions between artists, collectors, and enthusiasts. Be active in related online forums and communities to network with like-minded individuals who can offer advice or feedback. This will help you stay informed about trends or opportunities while ensuring that others pay attention when you launch your NFTs.

In conclusion, creating successful NFTs demands careful planning and execution in both design and marketing. By focusing on quality, originality, engaging metadata, and community outreach, you'll be well on your way to carving out a unique place for yourself in the world of digital art ownership.

Navigating the World of NFTs: Identifying Your Niche and Target Market

Here are some tips for finding your niche and pinpointing your target market.

Understanding NFT Niches

NFT niches are often associated with specific types of digital assets, such as artwork, collectable cards, virtual real estate, in-game items, or intellectual property rights. When determining your niche, consider the following:

1. Passion: Choose a niche that you're passionate about or have experience in. This will make it easier for you to create engaging content, establish credibility in the space, and connect with like-minded collectors and enthusiasts.

2. Demand: Research existing NFT collections, marketplaces, and trends to get a sense of what's currently in demand. Pay attention to which themes, styles, or genres are getting traction and consider how you can put a unique twist on them.

3. Scarcity: Identifying niches with limited supply or competition increases the potential value of your NFTs. Explore less saturated markets where your digital assets can stand out and garner attention.

Identifying Your Target Market

Now that you've identified your niche, it's essential to hone in on your target market — the specific group of people who are most likely to be interested in your NFTs. Keep these factors in mind:

1. Demographics: Consider age, gender, location, income level, and interests when defining your target audience. These factors will influence not only the type of NFTs you create but also your marketing and outreach strategies.

2. Motivations: Understand the motivations of potential buyers, whether they're collectors looking to add to their digital art portfolios, gamers seeking in-game advantages, or investors hoping to capitalize on NFT

trends. Tailor your NFTs and messaging to address these motivations.

3. Community Engagement: Join social media platforms, forums, and chat groups focused on your niche to connect with potential buyers. Create engaging content that showcases your NFTs and builds excitement around your brand.

4. Influencer Collaborations: Partner with influencers within your niche who have an established following. They can help promote your NFTs and provide valuable exposure to a wider audience.

With a clear understanding of your niche and target market, you can create exclusive NFTs that resonate with your audience and stand out amidst the competition. By anticipating market demand, offering unique value propositions, and targeting the right audience, you will be well-positioned to make an impact in the exciting world of non-fungible tokens.

Creating a Unique Value Proposition for NFTs: Standing Out in the Digital Art World

These digital assets have revolutionized the way we buy, sell, and trade digital art. But, with thousands of NFTs entering the market every day, it has become increasingly challenging to make your NFT stand out. In this section, we'll discuss how you can create a unique value proposition (UVP) for your NFTs to attract collectors and make your digital art more valuable.

1. Understand Your Target Audience

When creating a UVP, it's crucial to understand who you want to attract with your NFT artwork. Are your target buyers serious collectors or casual enthusiasts? By understanding their interests, motivations, and preferences, you can tailor your NFT's narrative and aesthetics to resonate with them.

2. Develop a Compelling Story

A powerful narrative is essential if you want your NFT to capture the attention of potential buyers. This story could be about the creative process behind your artwork or its inspiration from real-life events or popular culture. By connecting your artwork to something relatable and interesting for your target audience, you increase its appeal.

3. Incorporate Scarcity

One key aspect of NFTs that makes them valuable is their scarcity. Limiting the supply of your digital art pieces can create demand among collectors and increase their worth. Consider issuing a limited number of editions or even creating one-of-a-kind pieces. By doing so, you create a sense of urgency among potential buyers and underscore your commitment to producing unique works.

4. Emphasize Quality

It's crucial to emphasize the quality of your artwork when promoting an NFT. High-quality visuals, including intricate details and innovative designs, can set your NFT apart from the competition. In addition, utilizing cutting-edge technology such as 3D rendering or virtual reality can create a more immersive and memorable experience for potential buyers.

5. Establish Your Digital Identity

Building a strong online presence is essential to increase your NFT's visibility and attract potential buyers. Showcase your digital art portfolio on social media platforms, Discord channels, or dedicated NFT forums. By engaging with other artists and collectors in these spaces, you increase your credibility and reputation, both of which are vital when selling NFTs.

6. Offer Additional Value

Adding additional value to your NFT is an effective way to set yourself apart from other artists. Consider offering exclusive benefits or experiences for holders of your NFTs, such as access to special events, behind-the-scenes content, or even physical rewards like signed prints or merchandise. By doing so, you strengthen your UVP and encourage more people to invest in your work.

Creating a unique value proposition for your NFTs is critical in today's crowded digital art market. By understanding your target audience, crafting a compelling narrative around your artwork, emphasizing quality and scarcity, building an online presence, and offering extra perks or exclusivity, you can stand out among the competition and attract the attention of avid collectors.

Creating digital art assets

Design principles for NFTs

Creating Digital Art Assets: Design Principles for NFTs

The world of digital art is booming. It's essential to understand the design principles that make your work stand out and thrive in this highly competitive space. Here are some key design principles to keep in mind when creating digital art assets for NFTs.

1. Uniqueness

To create a successful NFT, ensure that your digital art asset is one-of-a-kind. Uniqueness is a crucial factor that draws potential buyers and collectors in the NFT market. Focus on developing innovative concepts and original designs that set your artwork apart from others in the market.

2. Aesthetic Appeal

Your digital art asset should be visually appealing to capture the interest of potential buyers. Pay attention to elements like color scheme, composition, and overall design; they contribute significantly to the aesthetic appeal of your work. Additionally, ensure you have an engaging visual style that resonates with your target audience.

3. Storytelling

To make your digital art asset truly memorable, it should tell a story or evoke emotions within its audience. Think about the narrative you want to communicate through your artwork, whether it's a personal expression or a broader interpretation of a subject matter. Your storytelling ability will add depth and meaning to your creation, making it more valuable as an NFT.

4. Technical Execution

The technical aspect of creating digital art assets for NFTs is crucial for their success in the market. Ensure that you master various software and tools used in digital art creation processes to produce high-quality and polished final pieces. Also, optimize the file sizes and resolutions to ensure proper viewing on various devices without compromising quality.

5. Adherence to Platform Guidelines

Various NFT marketplaces have specific guidelines and requirements for digital art assets. Familiarize yourself with these guidelines and ensure that your artwork conforms to them. This helps prevent any potential complications or issues when listing your NFTs.

6. Scope for Customization and Updates

The NFT market is constantly evolving, so consider creating digital art assets that can be customized or updated over time. This adds a layer of value to your NFT and can attract buyers interested in owning dynamic and evolving digital art pieces.

In conclusion, understanding the design principles and being able to apply them effectively is crucial in creating digital art assets specifically for NFTs.

By focusing on uniqueness, aesthetic appeal, storytelling, technical execution, platform guidelines adherence, and scope for customization, you'll create engaging and high-quality digital art pieces that stand out in the competitive NFT market.

Navigating the World of NFTs: Top File Formats to Consider

These unique tokens, built on blockchain technology, have revolutionized the way creators can monetize and authenticate their digital assets. However, not all file formats are suitable for use as NFTs. In this section, we will delve into the best file formats that are ideal for NFT creation.

1. PNG and JPEG: Preserving the Beauty of Your Digital Images

For digital images and artwork, PNG (Portable Network Graphics) and JPEG (Joint Photographic Experts Group) are the two most popular file formats. Both of these formats are widely accepted across various NFT marketplaces and platforms, making them a reliable choice for creators.

PNG is a lossless compression format, perfect for preserving intricate details and vibrant colours in your artwork. This format supports transparency, which can be an essential factor for some digital artists.

On the other hand, JPEG is a lossy compression format that sacrifices some image quality in exchange for smaller file sizes. This format is suitable for NFTs with more complex artwork or photographs that require less precise detail preservation.

2. GIF: Breathe Life into Your NFTs with Motion

The Graphic Interchange Format (GIF) is an excellent option for creators looking to add animation or motion to their NFTs. The GIF format is widely supported on social media platforms, making it easier to promote your animated tokens across various channels.

Though limited in colour depth compared to other image formats, its ability to loop sequences seamlessly and create engaging animations makes GIF an appealing choice for NFT collectors.

3. MP4 and WebM: Video Formats for Immersive Digital Experiences

Incorporating video into your NFT can create immersive experiences for your audience. The two most popular video formats for NFTs are MP4 (MPEG-4 Part 14) and WebM.

MP4 accommodates both video and audio tracks, as well as text overlays, making it a versatile choice. Its lossy compression ensures that videos remain high-quality while maintaining smaller file sizes. This format is supported across multiple devices and platforms.

WebM, on the other hand, is an open-source, royalty-free format designed specifically for web use. While not as widely supported as MP4, WebM offers efficient compression and streaming capabilities suitable for digital art with video components.

4. GLB: The Future of NFTs in 3D

For creators looking to venture into the world of 3D digital art and collectables, the GLB (GL Transmission Format Binary) file format is arguably the best choice for NFTs. This format accommodates 3D models and animations while supporting real-time rendering capabilities.

Platforms like Decentraland and Somnium Space utilize GLB files to offer virtual reality experiences where users can showcase and trade their immersive NFT masterpieces.

In conclusion, selecting the appropriate file format for your NFT plays a crucial role in how it's experienced by collectors.

Whether it's a high-resolution image in PNG or JPEG format, an engaging animation in GIF format, a captivating video rendered in MP4 or WebM, or an immersive 3D experience using GLB files – choosing the right format can amplify your digital artwork's appeal in the competitive world of NFTs.

Writing the code for NFTs

Overview of Ethereum blockchain and smart contracts

Demystifying the World of NFTs: Writing Code for Non-Fungible Tokens on the Ethereum Blockchain

At the core of this technological innovation lies the Ethereum blockchain and its versatile smart contracts. In this section, we'll dive into the fundamentals of writing code for NFTs while exploring an overview of the Ethereum blockchain and smart contracts.

Understanding the Ethereum Blockchain

Before we delve into coding NFTs, it's essential to familiarize ourselves with the Ethereum blockchain. Launched in 2015, Ethereum is an open-source, decentralized platform that enables developers to build and deploy smart contracts. These self-executing contracts contain code that automatically enforces specific terms and conditions upon all parties involved in a transaction.

Ethereum not only supports cryptocurrency transactions but fuels a wide range of decentralized applications (dApps). It is the underlying technology behind the creation and management of NFTs.

Exploring Smart Contracts

At the heart of every NFT transaction is a smart contract. Written in Solidity (a programming language specifically designed for Ethereum), these contracts define rules, attributes, and functionality for digital assets such as ownership, transferability, and metadata.

Writing code for NFTs

To create your first NFT, follow these steps:

1. Install development tools: Begin by installing Node.js on your computer, followed by Truffle – a popular development framework that streamlines contract creation.

2. Set up your project: Using Truffle's built-in commands or templates (called "boxes"), initiate a new project.

3. Write your smart contract: Draw inspiration from existing resources like OpenZeppelin – an open-source library brimming with vetted and community-reviewed smart contract templates – to construct an ERC-721 (a common token standard for NFTs) contract. Your contract should outline attributes such as:

  - The token's name and symbol

  - A function to "mint" or create new NFTs

  - Ownership transfer mechanisms

4. Deploy your smart contract: Upon refining and finalizing your code, deploy your smart contract to the Ethereum blockchain for testing using a local development environment like Ganache. This step simulates mining transactions, allowing you to test the functionality of your NFT.

5. Test your NFT: Utilize Truffle's testing tools to confirm the proper execution of your contract's functions.

6. Deploy onto a live Ethereum network: When satisfied with your project's performance, migrate it onto a live Ethereum network (like Rinkeby, a widely-used test network). This step is crucial for ensuring your NFT operates seamlessly in real-world scenarios before officially launching.

Intermediate Guide to Designing NFTs

Final Thoughts

Writing code for NFTs can be an exciting and fulfilling journey that sheds light on the fascinating world of digital art and collectables. By understanding the workings of the Ethereum blockchain and smart contracts, even novice developers can get a taste of this burgeoning technological landscape. Keep in mind that patience, practice, and continuous learning are crucial to mastering the art of coding for NFTs – but with dedication, the possibilities are limitless!

Unlocking the World of Ethereum: An In-Depth Guide to Understanding the Blockchain and Accessing Its Capabilities

Ethereum, a cutting-edge innovation in the world of blockchain technology, has captivated the interest of both tech enthusiasts and general audiences alike. But what exactly is Ethereum, and how does it operate? In this comprehensive guide, we'll delve into the inner workings of Ethereum, explain its key features, and provide insights on how to access its vast potential.

What is Ethereum?

Ethereum is an open-source, decentralized blockchain platform that allows developers to create and deploy smart contracts and decentralized applications (dApps). Serving as an extension to the initial concept of blockchain introduced by Bitcoin, it aims to provide diverse functionality beyond just hosting a digital currency. Ethereum has its own cryptocurrency known as Ether (ETH), which is used as a means for exchanging value and paying for transaction fees.

How Does Ethereum Blockchain Work?

Ethereum operates using a distributed ledger technology called blockchain. When transactions occur within the network, they are grouped into blocks. Each block contains transaction data and is cryptographically linked to the preceding one in a chronological chain. This ensures transparency and security since once data has been recorded; it cannot be retroactively altered without altering subsequent blocks.

The driving force behind Ethereum's operation is smart contracts – self-executing agreements written with lines of code that automatically enforce contract terms without intermediaries. These smart contracts are stored on the blockchain and allow for trustless transactions between parties while eliminating risks associated with fraud or defaulting parties.

Moreover, Ethereum employs a consensus algorithm called Proof-of-

Stake (PoS) - a more environmentally friendly alternative to Bitcoin's Proof-of-Work (PoW). Validators in PoS hold cryptocurrency deposits as stakes that validate transactions instead of solving complex mathematical problems found in PoW mining operations.

Accessing the Ethereum Blockchain

To interact with the blockchain, you'll start with setting up an Ethereum wallet. Some popular options include MetaMask, MyEtherWallet, and hardware wallets like Ledger or Trezor. These wallets let you store Ether and ERC-20 tokens, manage your portfolio, and interact with decentralized applications within the Ethereum ecosystem.

Next, you'll need to acquire some Ether to fund transactions or engage with dApps. You can either mine Ether yourself or purchase it on a cryptocurrency exchange using other digital assets or fiat currency.

Finally, explore the world of decentralized applications that run on the Ethereum platform. There's an extensive range of dApps available in various industries, such as finance, gaming, and IoT. Simply connect your Ethereum wallet to access these innovative tools and make transactions securely.

In conclusion, Ethereum offers a versatile and dynamic blockchain network that expands the original vision of blockchain technology. With its core features of smart contracts and dApps, Ethereum provides a new landscape for developers and users alike to create secure decentralized solutions. Embrace the world of Ethereum by setting up your wallet, acquiring Ether, and engaging with its vast ecosystem – welcome to the future of decentralization!

Solidity syntax and features for NFT development

ERC-721 standard for non-fungible tokens

ERC-1155 standard for multiple token types

Unlocking the Power of NFT Development: Exploring Solidity Syntax and Features for ERC-721 and ERC-1155 Standards

One of the key technologies driving this wave of innovation is Solidity – a powerful programming language designed specifically for developing smart contracts on the Ethereum blockchain. To harness the full potential of NFTs, it's essential to understand Solidity syntax and features, as well as the ERC-721 and ERC-1155 token standards. This section will delve into these topics to provide you with a comprehensive understanding of NFT development.

An Introduction to Solidity Syntax

Solidity is a statically-typed, contract-oriented language designed with Ethereum in mind. Drawing inspiration from languages like C++, Python, and JavaScript, Solidity provides a familiar syntax that allows developers to create powerful smart contracts. Its syntax includes variables, functions, control structures (e.g., if/else, loops), and classes (called 'contracts' in Solidity).

The foundation for any Solidity contract is its state variables and functions. State variables are used to store data on the blockchain while functions define the contract's behavior and can modify state variables. Functions can be further classified into public, private, internal, or external based on their visibility. Developers also make use of events and modifiers to manage function execution.

ERC-721: Non-Fungible Token Standard

The ERC-721 standard has emerged as the most popular standard for non-fungible tokens (NFTs). It defines a set of rules that govern how unique tokens are created, transferred, and managed within a smart contract. The primary functions associated with this standard include:

1. mint(): Used to create new tokens.

Intermediate Guide to Designing NFTs

2. burn(): Destroys a token when no longer needed.

3. ownerOf(): Determines the owner of a given token.

4. balanceOf(): Displays the number of tokens owned by a specific address.

5. transferFrom(): Facilitates the transfer of tokens between two addresses.

By implementing this standard, developers can create individual tokens that represent unique assets, such as digital art, real estate, or collectibles.

ERC-1155: The Multi-Token Standard

While the ERC-721 standard focuses on non-fungible tokens, the ERC-1155 standard combines both fungible and non-fungible token features within a single contract. This hybrid approach enables developers to create multiple token types with varying levels of uniqueness and rarity under one contract. Key features of ERC-1155 include:

1. batchMint(): Allows the creation of multiple tokens at once.

2. batchBurn(): Destroys multiple tokens simultaneously.

3. balanceOf(): Functions similarly to ERC-721 but accounts for multiple token types.

4. safeBatchTransferFrom(): Enables transferring multiple tokens between different addresses securely.

Adopting the ERC-1155 standard can lead to increased efficiency and versatility for projects that require managing a diverse range of token types.

In conclusion, mastering Solidity syntax and understanding the features associated with ERC-721 and ERC-1155 standards are crucial to fueling innovation in NFT development. As more creators, collectors, and businesses explore this exciting new frontier, it's paramount that developers stay ahead of the curve by broadening their skills in these essential areas. By doing so, they'll bring forth new opportunities in this rapidly growing ecosystem while unlocking the true power NFTs have to offer.

Demystifying the ERC-721 Standard: The Backbone of Non-Fungible Tokens (NFTs)

The meteoric rise of non-fungible tokens (NFTs) in the blockchain ecosystem has drawn the spotlight to ERC-721, the standard that powers these unique digital assets. As a token standard, ERC-721 facilitates the creation and management of NFTs within the Ethereum ecosystem. In this section, we will provide a detailed exploration of the ERC-721 standard, highlighting its significance and importance in the world of NFTs.

A Brief Overview of Token Standards

Before diving into ERC-721, it's crucial to understand token standards in general. Token standards are guidelines that define how tokens should be created, transferred, and managed on a blockchain. Ethereum-based tokens follow established standards, such as ERC-20 for fungible tokens and, in our case, ERC-721 for non-fungible tokens.

Understanding Non-Fungible Tokens

Non-fungible tokens represent one-of-a-kind digital assets with unique attributes that differentiate them from other NFTs - think rare art, collectibles or virtual real estate. Unlike fungible tokens like cryptocurrencies (which are interchangeable), each NFT is distinct and cannot be exchanged at a one-to-one ratio.

As a result, NFTs require a token standard tailored to their characteristics —enter ERC-721.

The Core Features of ERC-721

As a token standard designed explicitly for non-fungible tokens, ERC-721 has several features that set it apart from other token standards:

1. Uniqueness: Each ERC-721 token is assigned a distinct identification number called a "token ID." This unique identifier ensures that each token remains distinguishable from others within its contract.

2. Ownership: The ERC-721 standard enables clear identification of an NFT's owner by mapping token IDs to owner addresses. This functionality allows straightforward transfer and secure management of digital assets.

3. Metadata: Extensible metadata features enable ERC-721 tokens to store additional information such as images, descriptions, or other attributes, adding contextual richness to each NFT.

4. Interoperability: The standardized nature of ERC-721 tokens ensures their compatibility across various wallets, marketplaces, and dApps, which simplifies usability for both developers and users.

ERC-721 Use Cases

Ethereum's ERC-721 standard has paved the way for an array of innovative applications in the NFT space:

- Digital art and collectibles: Projects like CryptoKitties and CryptoPunks leverage ERC-721 tokens to create unique digital art assets with verifiable ownership and scarcity.

- Virtual real estate: Platforms such as Decentraland use ERC-721 tokens to represent virtual land parcels, granting owners property rights within a virtual world.

- Intellectual property: Content creators can mint NFTs for their work (music, books, or videos), enabling proof of ownership and opening opportunities for direct monetization.

In Conclusion

The ERC-721 standard has ushered in a new era of blockchain innovation centered around non-fungible tokens. By providing a robust framework for creating, managing, and transferring unique digital assets on the Ethereum network, ERC-721 has contributed significantly to the adoption and popularity of NFTs in various domains.

As this technology continues to evolve, it's exciting to envision the endless possibilities that may emerge from creative applications built on top of this ground-breaking standard.

An In-Depth Look at the ERC-1155 Standard: Revolutionizing Token Diversity in the Blockchain World

The Ethereum blockchain has evolved considerably since its inception, with various token standards emerging to address specific use cases. Among these innovations, the ERC-1155 standard stands out for its ability to manage multiple token types within a single smart contract. This unique feature has far-reaching implications for the world of cryptocurrencies, NFTs, and beyond. Let's delve into the intricacies of the ERC-1155 standard and explore its potential impact on the blockchain ecosystem.

Understanding the ERC-1155 Standard

Developed by Enjin's team in 2018, the ERC-1155 standard revolutionized token management by combining the best features of existing standards, such as ERC-20 (fungible tokens) and ERC-721 (non-fungible tokens). Unlike its predecessors, the ERC-1155 allows for the creation and management of both fungible and non-fungible tokens within a single smart contract.

The core advantage of this multi-token approach lies in its efficiency. By bundling multiple token types under one contract, users can perform batch transactions, thereby reducing gas fees and enhancing overall performance. This efficiency is particularly significant in industries such as gaming, where various token types are often used simultaneously.

Fungible and Non-Fungible Tokens: The Key Differences

Before diving deeper into the benefits of the ERC-1155 standard, it's essential to understand the fundamental differences between fungible and non-fungible tokens.

Fungible tokens are interchangeable and hold equal value. For example, one Bitcoin is valued equally to another Bitcoin. The most popular fungible token standard is ERC-20.

On the other hand, non-fungible tokens (NFTs) possess unique properties that make them irreplaceable and distinct from one another. For instance, digital art or in-game items fall under NFTs, as each piece has distinct characteristics. The most widely-adopted non-fungible token standard is ERC-721.

The Potential Impact of the ERC-1155 Standard

By enabling the creation and management of multiple token types within one contract, the ERC-1155 standard unlocks numerous possibilities for various industries:

1. Gaming: In-game assets often require both fungible and non-fungible tokens to be used simultaneously. The ERC-1155 allows developers to create more immersive gaming experiences by streamlining in-game economies and simplifying asset/token transfers.

2. Decentralized Finance (DeFi): The DeFi ecosystem relies heavily on fungible tokens for governance, liquidity provision, and other functions. With the addition of non-fungible tokens through the ERC-1155 standard, DeFi protocols can further diversify their offerings and explore new use cases.

3. Digital Art and Collectibles: The ERC-1155 standard presents opportunities for creating intricate digital art collections that combine both fungible and non-fungible elements.

4. Supply Chain Management: By using multiple token types, companies can efficiently track and manage assets at different levels of granularity across their supply chain networks.

In conclusion, the ERC-1155 token standard presents an innovative approach to managing multiple token types within a single smart contract. Its ability to streamline operations involving both fungible and non-fungible tokens opens up a world of possibilities for various industries within the blockchain ecosystem. As more developers begin to harness this powerful technology, we can expect to see a greater diversity of applications and use cases emerge in the near future.

Developing a Custom Smart Contract for Your NFT Project: A Comprehensive Guide

To successfully launch an NFT project, developing a custom smart contract is crucial. In this detailed guide, we'll cover the essential steps to creating a personalized smart contract for your NFT endeavour.

1. Understand the Basics

Before diving into the development process, familiarize yourself with the core concepts of blockchain technology and how NFTs work. Knowledge of Ethereum's ERC-721 and ERC-1155 token standards is especially beneficial, as they serve as the basis for creating NFTs.

2. Choose a Blockchain Platform

Select an appropriate blockchain platform for your NFT project. Though Ethereum is the most popular choice due to its widespread adoption and versatility, alternatives like Binance Smart Chain, Flow, and Tezos are also worth exploring based on your specific needs and preferences.

3. Set Up Your Development Environment

To start building your NFT smart contract, set up an appropriate development environment:

 - Install software tools like Node.js, Git, Truffle Framework, and Ganache.
 - Configure the Metamask browser extension to manage test wallets.

4. Write Your Smart Contract

Utilizing a programming language such as Solidity or Vyper, write your smart contract based on the ERC-721 or ERC-1155 standard. Key aspects to consider during this stage include:

 - Token Metadata: Define how each NFT's unique attributes will be stored and accessed.

Intermediate Guide to Designing NFTs

- Transfer Mechanics: Implement functions that enable users to transfer or trade their tokens.

- Minting Logic: Determine how new NFTs will be created within your ecosystem.

- Access Control: Set roles and permissions for administrative tasks like minting tokens or updating metadata.

5. Test Your Smart Contract

Thoroughly test your smart contract to ensure the correct implementation of all intended features and to detect any potential vulnerabilities. Take advantage of testing frameworks like Truffle to simulate blockchain interactions and perform unit tests on your functions.

6. Deploy Your Smart Contract

Once your smart contract is fully tested and optimized, deploy it to the chosen blockchain network using a tool such as Truffle Migrations or Remix IDE. Be sure to review gas costs and consider optimizations to minimize transaction fees for users.

7. Build Your NFT Marketplace

As a final step, create an intuitive user interface for your NFT platform, allowing users to interact with your smart contract easily. Developing a robust marketplace portal will ensure seamless token browsing, purchasing, and trading experiences for your community.

By following these steps, you'll be well on your way to crafting a custom smart contract specifically tailored to your NFT project's unique requirements. Remember that ongoing monitoring and maintenance are necessary for ensuring the long-term success of your token ecosystem.

Testing and deploying your NFT smart contract on the Ethereum network

Local testing using Truffle and Ganache

Testing and Deploying Your Smart Contract on the Ethereum Network

With NFTs offering verifiable digital ownership and unique properties, artists and collectors worldwide are keen to get on board. But before you can start minting your own NFTs, it's essential to understand the process of testing and deploying your smart contract on the Ethereum network. In this section, we'll delve into the details, equipping you with the knowledge needed to launch your very own NFT endeavour.

1. Developing Your Smart Contract

The first step in creating an NFT is developing a smart contract that conforms to the ERC-721 token standard, which defines a set of rules for non-fungible tokens on Ethereum. This typically involves utilizing a programming language like Solidity and employing development tools like Truffle or Remix. It's crucial to ensure that your contract encompasses all necessary functions, such as minting tokens, transferring ownership, and enumerating tokens held by an address.

2. Testing Your Contract

Once you've written your smart contract, thorough testing is imperative to ensure its functionality and security. This process involves deploying your contract on a local or test blockchain network like Ganache or Ropsten. Several testing frameworks exist with which you can write test suites; these include Truffle (for JavaScript), Brownie (for Python), and Waffle (for TypeScript). Tests should cover all aspects of your smart contract functionality, including token creation, value assignment, error handling, and user permissions.

3. Deploying Your Contract

With the smart contract tested extensively and proven functional, it's now time for deployment on the Ethereum mainnet.

Before deployment, double-check that your contract is optimized for gas usage since every code execution on Ethereum consumes gas – a scarce resource, measured in Gwei, with prices subject to market fluctuations. Gas price optimization is crucial to ensure that your NFT project remains cost-effective for users.

Deploying a contract often involves running a migration script through a command-line interface. The most popular methods include using Truffle, Hardhat, or manually deploying using Solidity via Remix and MetaMask. When deployment is complete, your smart contract will obtain a unique address on Ethereum mainnet, signifying that it's now live and ready for interaction.

4. Verifying and Auditing Your Contract

After deployment comes the critical step of verification: a process by which you share the contract source code on a blockchain explorer like Etherscan to demonstrate its legitimacy to the public. Verification allows users to obtain a clear understanding of your token's functions and working mechanisms.

Additionally, consider engaging an external auditing firm to conduct a thorough security analysis of your smart contract. This ensures that any security vulnerabilities are addressed, lending credibility to your NFT project and instilling confidence among potential investors and users.

In conclusion, testing and deploying your NFT smart contract on the Ethereum network is an intricate yet rewarding process. By following these steps and adopting best practices, you'll be well on your way to establishing a foothold in the fast-paced realm of digital collectables.

Mastering Local Testing with Truffle: A Comprehensive Guide

In the world of blockchain development, having a reliable and efficient testing environment is crucial. That's where Truffle comes in – a development framework designed specifically for Ethereum-based projects. With Truffle, developers can test and deploy smart contracts, manage networks, and perform various tasks with ease.

1. Install Truffle and Ganache

Before we dive into testing, make sure you have both Truffle and Ganache installed on your system. Truffle is the development framework, while Ganache is a personal blockchain that allows you to run tests, execute commands, and inspect state while controlling the chain's operation.

To install Truffle globally on your machine, run the following command:

```
```

```
npm install -g truffle
```

```
```

To install Ganache, visit their official website at https://www.trufflesuite.com/ganache and download the appropriate version for your operating system.

2. Initialize a New Project with Truffle

Create a new directory for your project and navigate to it in your terminal. Then, run the following command to initialize a new Truffle project:

```
```

```
truffle init
```

```
```

This will generate a basic project structure with default configuration files and example contracts.

3. Configure Your Project

Next, you need to configure your project to connect with Ganache as your local blockchain provider. Open the `truffle-config.js` file in your project directory and modify it as follows:

```javascript
module.exports = {
  networks: {
    development: {
      host: "127.0.0.1",
      port: 7545,
      network_id: "*" // Match any network ID
    }
  },
  // ...
};
```

Ensure that the `host` and `port` values match your Ganache client's settings.

4. Write Your Smart Contract

Create a new Solidity file (*.sol) in the `contracts` folder of your project and write your smart contract following the Solidity syntax and conventions.

5. Write Your Test Cases

Create a new JavaScript file (*.js) in the `test` folder of your project, and write your test cases using Truffle's testing framework, which is based on Mocha and Chai.

6. Execute Your Tests

With everything set up properly, it's time to execute your test cases. In your terminal, navigate to your project directory and run the following command:

```
truffle test
```

Truffle will compile your contracts, deploy them to your local Ganache blockchain, and execute the test cases you have written. You can view the results of all tests directly in the terminal.

7. Refine and Iterate

After completing your tests, you can refine your smart contract code or tests based on the results obtained. Conduct more tests as needed to ensure the reliability and security of your smart contracts.

By utilizing Truffle's powerful testing capabilities combined with Ganache's personal blockchain environment, developers can greatly improve their Ethereum-based projects' quality. With this guide as a starting point, you'll be well on your way to mastering local testing for blockchain development using Truffle.

Mastering Local Testing with Ganache: A Comprehensive Guide

One of the tools that are essential for any blockchain developer's toolkit is Ganache - a local testing environment for Ethereum-based applications. In this section, we'll take a deep dive into Ganache, helping you understand its importance and guide you through its various features to efficiently test your DApps locally.

What is Ganache?

Ganache is a personal Ethereum blockchain designed for local testing of smart contracts and decentralized applications. It allows developers to deploy contracts, develop DApps, and run tests without worrying about the cost associated with deploying to the main Ethereum network or other testnets. Since Ganache operates in a sandboxed environment, it provides a safe space where you can experiment without affecting the main chain or losing real Ether.

Why Use Ganache?

Ganache offers several advantages that make it an essential tool for developing and testing on the Ethereum platform:

1. Instant mining: While public testnets require you to wait for your transactions to be mined, Ganache instantly mines each transaction.

2. Control over accounts: Ganache provides a set of pre-funded accounts (typically 10), each loaded with 100 Ether by default. This allows you to test your DApps without dealing with real Ether or requesting tokens from faucets in public testnets.

3. Customizable settings: You can configure block times, network IDs,

gas limits, and hard forks according to your requirements, ensuring that your tests will run smoothly.

4. Superior debugging: Ganache provides a wealth of information about transactions and events that occur within the environment, making it easy to debug any issues during development.

5. Integration with popular development frameworks: You can effortlessly integrate Ganache with popular development frameworks like Truffle Suite, making it a one-stop testing solution for your DApps.

How to Get Started with Ganache?

Ganache is available in two forms: Ganache CLI and Ganache GUI. The CLI version can be installed using npm (Node Package Manager) with the following command:

```
```

npm install -g ganache-cli

```
```

Once installed, you can simply run `ganache-cli` in your terminal to start it.

On the other hand, you can download the GUI version from the official website (https://www.trufflesuite.com/ganache), compatible with Windows, macOS, and Linux. Launch the application and create a new workspace to get started.

Using Ganache for Local Testing

Once your Ganache environment is up and running, you can begin interacting with it using your preferred method - be it CLI or GUI.

1. Deploying Contracts: You can use tools like Truffle Suite or Remix IDE to deploy your smart contracts on the local network. Make sure to set the correct network settings (RPC server and network ID) to connect to your Ganache instance.

2. Execute Transactions: Your DApps can send transactions and interact with deployed smart contracts as if they were on a public testnet or mainnet.

3. Analyze Blockchain Data: With Ganache, you can analyze transaction details, events fired by contracts, view balance changes in accounts, and monitor gas usage for every transaction. This helps identify bottlenecks and optimize your code for better performance.

Conclusion

Local testing with Ganache is crucial for ensuring the flawless functionality and security of your Ethereum-based decentralized applications before deploying them on the mainnet. Its ease of use and powerful features make it an indispensable tool for any Ethereum developer looking to build innovative solutions for the world of blockchain technology.

Deploying Smart Contracts on Public Testnets: A Guide to Ropsten, Rinkeby, and More

As the world of decentralized applications (dApps) and blockchain technology continues to expand, building and testing projects on Ethereum's network has become increasingly essential. In this section, we will discuss the importance of deploying smart contracts on public testnets like Ropsten and Rinkeby, detailing the process for a seamless experience.

Understanding Public Testnets

Public testnets are essential for developers due to many reasons. These test environments mimic the Ethereum blockchain's environment, features, and functionality but without requiring real Ether for transactions. This setup allows developers to test their dApps and smart contracts before deployment on the mainnet, reducing errors and ensuring the project functions as intended.

Intermediate Guide to Designing NFTs

Main Ethereum Test Networks

There are several public Ethereum testnets available; however, Ropsten and Rinkeby are among the most popular choices. Each of these networks has its unique characteristics.

1. Ropsten - As a proof-of-work (PoW) based testnet, Ropsten is quite similar to Ethereum's main network (mainnet). This makes it suitable for testing transactions and contract deployments with similar conditions to the mainnet. However, this also means it is susceptible to spam attacks leading to potential instability.

2. Rinkeby - In contrast to Ropsten, Rinkeby is a proof-of-authority (PoA) based testnet that only allows verified authorities to validate transactions. This network offers better stability but lacks similarity in consensus algorithms with the main Ethereum network.

Deploying Smart Contracts on Public Testnets

Before you begin deploying your smart contract on a public testnet, consider the following steps:

1. Acquire Test Ether - To deploy and interact with your smart contract on a testnet, you need its respective cryptocurrency. For this purpose, visit

Intermediate Guide to Designing NFTs

an Ethereum faucet like Ropsten Faucet or Rinkeby Faucet to obtain test Ether.

2. Set Up MetaMask - To deploy your smart contract using a test network, you first need a wallet that supports those networks, like MetaMask. Install the MetaMask browser extension and connect it to the desired testnet.

3. Migrate Your Smart Contract - Use a development framework like Truffle to migrate your smart contract. Update the Truffle configuration file to reference the corresponding test network and your MetaMask wallet address.

4. Deploy Your Smart Contract - With Truffle configured correctly, navigate to your terminal and enter "truffle migrate --network <network-name>". Replace <network-name> with Ropsten or Rinkeby depending on your chosen testnet. This action will deploy your smart contract to the specified test network.

5. Test Your Smart Contract - Once deployed, interact and test your smart contract's functionality using Remix IDE or any other tool that supports communication with Ethereum's public networks.

Conclusion

Deploying smart contracts on public testnets is a critical step for any Ethereum developer. By understanding the use of Ropsten, Rinkeby, and other testnets, you can safely deploy and thoroughly vet your projects before eventually transitioning them to the main Ethereum network, ensuring stability, correctness, and reduced risks for potential users.

Deploying to the Ethereum Mainnet: A Comprehensive Guide

The Ethereum mainnet is the primary, public-facing blockchain that hosts decentralized applications (dApps) and various cryptocurrencies. For developers, deploying a smart contract or dApp on the Ethereum mainnet marks the culmination of their hard work, allowing their creations to be accessible and useful to users.

However, the deployment process can be complex and requires a strong grasp of various concepts. In this section, we'll guide you through a detailed explanation of deploying your smart contract or dApp on the Ethereum mainnet.

1. Understand the deployment process

Before diving into deployment, it's important to understand the overall process. In a simplified form, you'll start by writing your smart contract using Solidity programming language, testing and debugging it on local development environments (like Ganache) and testnets (such as Ropsten or Rinkeby). Once you're satisfied with its performance, you'll deploy it to the Ethereum mainnet.

2. Acquire Ether

You will need Ether (ETH) to pay for gas fees during deployment and for any subsequent transactions made on the mainnet. Gas fees are essentially the transaction costs required by Ethereum's network to execute your smart contract functions. You can acquire Ether through cryptocurrency exchanges or by mining.

3. Prepare your project files

Before deploying your project to the mainnet, ensure that all files are up to date and organized. This includes your Solidity code, configuration files detailing mainnet settings and addresses (such as truffle-config.js for Truffle projects), and any front-end web components that will interact with your smart contract.

4. Deploy using tools or frameworks

To deploy your smart contract or dApp on the Ethereum mainnet, you can use various tools and frameworks like Truffle, Hardhat, Remix IDE, among others. These tools streamline deployment by automating the compilation of Solidity code into bytecode and generating Application Binary Interfaces (ABIs), which allow your contract to communicate with the Ethereum network.

5. Verify and interact with your smart contract

After successfully deploying your smart contract or dApp, it's crucial to verify its behavior on the Ethereum mainnet. You can use tools like Etherscan to look up the transaction details and monitor your deployed contract. You may also interact with your smart contract using Web3 providers like MetaMask or custom-built front-end interfaces.

6. Optimize for gas efficiency

Since deploying and interacting with contracts on the Ethereum mainnet can be costly (due to gas fees), it's essential to optimize your code for gas efficiency. Eliminate unnecessary logic, reduce function calls, and minimize data storage requirements in your smart contracts as much as possible.

Intermediate Guide to Designing NFTs

7. Monitor updates and performance

After deploying your project on the Ethereum mainnet, you'll need to keep monitoring its performance and regularly update it in response to user feedback, security vulnerabilities, or regulatory requirements. Staying up-to-date with Ethereum's development is also crucial since network upgrades can potentially impact the operation of your smart contract or dApp.

In conclusion, deploying a smart contract or dApp on the Ethereum mainnet is a significant achievement for developers. By following these guidelines and best practices, you can ensure a smooth deployment process that leads to successful interaction with users on this popular blockchain platform.

Uploading and selling your NFTs on marketplaces

NFTs provide a unique way for creators to monetize their digital art by assigning ownership and value to their creations. If you're new to the NFT scene and looking to make your mark, this section will walk you through the process of uploading and selling your NFTs on popular marketplaces.

Uploading Your NFTs

The first step in selling your NFTs is to create and upload them to a marketplace. Here's how:

1. Mint your NFT: Before selling your work, you'll need to convert it into an NFT by minting it on a blockchain network, typically Ethereum. Various platforms, like OpenSea or Rarible, allow you to create an NFT by connecting your digital wallet (e.g., MetaMask) and uploading your digital file.

2. Add metadata: After uploading your file, include details like title, description, artist name, and other relevant information that potential buyers will find valuable. Good metadata enhances your NFT's visibility in search results and improves its chances of being discovered.

3. Set a price: Decide whether you want to sell your NFT via auction or at a fixed price. Carefully consider factors like the rarity of your creation and its perceived value when setting the price.

Popular Marketplaces

Several marketplaces specialize in the buying and selling of NFTs. Some popular options include:

1. OpenSea: As the largest NFT marketplace, OpenSea supports various

digital assets, including art, domain names, virtual real estate, and more. It's user-friendly and offers features like filtering options, advanced search functionality, and customizable storefronts.

2. Rarible: As a decentralized marketplace, Rarible enables artists to create and sell NFTs without intermediaries. Users can also earn RARI governance tokens through the platform's liquidity mining program.

3. SuperRare: Focusing on high-quality digital art, SuperRare is a curated platform that implements a stringent application process for both creators and collectors. This exclusivity means only a limited number of artists can access the platform at any given time.

4. Foundation: A relatively newer platform, Foundation connects creators with collectors through live auctions. It utilizes an invite-only system that ensures a certain level of prestige among its community.

Final Thoughts

Entering the world of NFTs can be both exciting and profitable when done correctly. However, it's essential to familiarize yourself with the ins and outs of minting, uploading, and selling your creations on popular marketplaces to maximize your chances of success. With diligent research and dedicated effort, you could soon turn your digital art into lucrative NFTs and establish yourself within this rapidly growing industry.

As the world of digital art and collectables continues to gain traction, non-fungible tokens (NFTs) are playing a major role in enabling artists and creators to monetize their work. For those looking to buy, sell, or trade NFTs, there are numerous online marketplaces designed specifically for this purpose. In this article, we'll explore some of the most popular NFT marketplaces currently available and provide their web addresses so you can start exploring these extraordinary platforms.

1. OpenSea (https://opensea.io/)

OpenSea is widely considered one of the largest and most versatile NFT marketplaces, showcasing artwork, collectables, domain names, tokenized real estate, virtual worlds, and more. With its user-friendly interface and extensive range of categories, OpenSea is an excellent starting point for both new and experienced NFT enthusiasts.

2. Rarible (https://rarible.com/)

Rarible is an NFT marketplace that caters especially to the creators of digital art and collectibles. This decentralized platform allows users to mint unique tokens for their creations while also supporting the buying and selling of such items. With a focus on user empowerment and rarity value, Rarible is an appealing choice for those interested in supporting independent creators.

3. SuperRare (https://superrare.co/)

As its name implies, SuperRare focuses on high-quality digital art from an exclusive selection of artists around the world. Known for its rigorous curation process that emphasizes rarity and uniqueness while advancing artistic narrative through the medium, SuperRare offers a prestigious marketplace for those who appreciate rare and cutting-edge digital art.

4. Foundation (https://foundation.app/)

Foundation's mission is to connect collectors with digital artists by providing a curated platform where users can engage in creating, collecting, and trading unique artworks. Through its slick design and sense of exclusiveness, Foundation has positioned itself as an attractive option for serious digital artists and collectors alike.

5. Nifty Gateway (https://niftygateway.com/)

Nifty Gateway is an NFT marketplace that specializes in limited edition, high-quality digital art and collectibles. Featuring a diverse range of themes and partnering with highly regarded artists, Nifty Gateway offers timed sales events called 'drops,' enabling collectors to acquire exclusive NFTs before they sell out.

6. Zora (https://zora.co/)

Zora is a decentralized NFT marketplace that focuses on creating new pricing models and pushing the envelope when it comes to tokenization possibilities. With its innovative approach, Zora is an interesting platform to watch as the NFT ecosystem continues to evolve.

7. BakerySwap (https://www.bakeryswap.org/)

BakerySwap is more than just an NFT marketplace – it's also a decentralized finance (DeFi) platform offering liquidity pools, yield farming, and other DeFi services. However, its built-in NFT section allows for the buying, selling, and creation of unique tokens within an exciting financial ecosystem.

As interest in NFTs continues to grow, so too will the number of marketplaces catering to this thriving digital art community. These popular platforms are just the beginning of a rapidly developing industry that promises to bring new opportunities for both creators and collectors alike.

From rare artworks to digital trading cards, NFT marketplaces have become the go-to platform for buying, selling, and trading these unique digital assets. If you're new to NFTs and looking to join the action, signing up and setting up an account on an NFT marketplace can seem daunting. But don't worry; we've got you covered! In this guide, we'll walk you through the process of creating an account on an NFT marketplace and linking your digital wallet.

Step 1: Choose an NFT Marketplace

Before you start, it's important to select a reputable NFT marketplace that supports the type of digital assets you're interested in. Some popular options include OpenSea, Rarible, SuperRare, and Foundation. Each platform has its unique features and community, so research each marketplace to see which one is best for your needs.

Step 2: Create Your Account

Once you've decided on a marketplace, head over to their website and create an account. Most NFT platforms would require basic information such as your name, email address, and a unique username or password. It's essential to use a secure password to protect your valuable digital assets from cyber threats.

Step 3: Set Up Your Digital Wallet

An integral part of interacting with the NFT market is setting up a compatible digital wallet. A digital wallet is essential for buying and selling NFTs as it securely stores your private keys and enables transactions on the blockchain.

Some widely-used wallets include MetaMask (for Ethereum-based NFTs), Trust Wallet (supports multiple blockchains), or Phantom (for Solana-based NFTs). To get started, download and install the appropriate wallet extension or app and create a new wallet by following the provided instructions.

Step 4: Fund Your Wallet

Before you can start purchasing NFTs, you'll need to add funds to your digital wallet. Depending on your NFT marketplace and the type of digital assets it supports, this could mean adding Ether (ETH), Solana (SOL), or other cryptocurrencies. To fund your wallet, you'd typically need to buy these cryptocurrencies through an exchange platform, such as Coinbase or Binance, and transfer them to your digital wallet.

Step 5: Link Your Wallet to the NFT Marketplace

With your account set up and funded, it's time to link your digital wallet to the NFT marketplace. Most platforms offer seamless wallet integration via browser extensions or QR codes. Navigate to your profile on the NFT marketplace and select the option to connect your wallet. Follow the prompts provided by the marketplace and approve any necessary transactions through your wallet. Once connected, you'll be able to view your balances and start exploring the world of NFTs.

By following these steps, you'll have successfully set up an account on an NFT marketplace and linked your digital wallet, opening up a world of unique digital art and collectables. Remember always to do thorough research before investing in any digital assets and use best practices when managing your account security.

Intermediate Guide to Designing NFTs

A Step-by-Step Guide to Setting Up Your MetaMask Wallet for NFTs and Digital Currencies

The need for a secure and user-friendly wallet to store your NFTs and cryptocurrencies is more crucial than ever. One of the most popular and trusted options available today is MetaMask, a browser extension that acts as your portal to the world of blockchain, allowing you to manage your digital assets with ease. If you're just getting started with MetaMask, this step-by-step guide will walk you through signing up and setting up your wallet.

Step 1: Download and Install MetaMask

MetaMask is available as an extension for popular web browsers like Chrome, Firefox, and Brave. To install MetaMask, visit their official website at metamask.io and click "Download Now." From there, choose the appropriate browser extension and follow the installation process for your specific web browser.

Step 2: Create a New MetaMask Wallet

Once you've installed the browser extension, you'll see the MetaMask fox logo in your browser's toolbar. Click on it to launch the setup process. You will be prompted to create a new wallet or import an existing one. For first-time users, select "Create a Wallet."

Intermediate Guide to Designing NFTs

Step 3: Choose a Strong Password

To ensure optimal security for your digital assets, create a strong password that's hard for others to guess. Your password should be unique and contain a mix of upper- and lower-case letters, numbers, and special characters. Once you've chosen your password, agree to the terms of use and click "Create."

Step 4: Back Up Your Secret Recovery Phrase

After creating a password, MetaMask will provide you with a 12-word secret recovery phrase. This phrase is vital for recovering your wallet if you ever forget your password or lose access to your device. Write this phrase down on paper or save it in a secure location that only you can access. Never share your recovery phrase with anyone, as it would compromise the security of your wallet.

Step 5: Confirm Your Secret Recovery Phrase

To ensure that you've correctly saved your recovery phrase, MetaMask will ask you to confirm it by selecting the words in the correct order. Once you've verified your phrase, click "Confirm."

Step 6: Start Exploring and Managing Your Digital Assets

With your MetaMask wallet set up, you're now ready to explore the world of NFTs and digital currencies. Use your wallet address to receive digital assets from others, connect to decentralized apps (dApps), and interact with various blockchain networks like Ethereum.

Step 7: Safely Store NFTs

When it comes to storing NFTs in your MetaMask wallet, ensure that it's connected to a marketplace or platform compatible with non-fungible tokens, like OpenSea or Rarible. Transfer your purchased or created NFTs to your MetaMask wallet address, and they will appear in the NFT section of your wallet once successfully transferred.

Remember to stay vigilant and protect your digital assets by keeping your password and recovery phrase secure. With these steps in mind, you're well on your way to managing and enjoying your NFTs and digital currencies with MetaMask.

When it comes to uploading digital art, proper formatting and adhering to metadata standards are crucial for ensuring your work is easily discoverable and shareable. In this step-by-step guide, we'll explore how to format your digital art for upload while maintaining metadata standards.

1. Choose the appropriate file format

Before uploading your digital art, it's essential to save it in the right file format. Common formats include JPEG, PNG, and GIF. JPEG is typically suitable for photos and images with lots of gradients, while PNG is better for images with transparency or sharp edges. GIFs are used for small animations.

2. Optimize your image resolution

Resolution plays a significant role in the quality of your uploaded digital art. A high-resolution image can display details clearly but could be slow to load on some devices or platforms. Aim for a balance between size and resolution, usually around 72 DPI (dots per inch) for web use.

3. Use descriptive file names

Naming your digital art files is an essential part of metadata organization. Make sure you include relevant keywords within the file name relating to the artwork's subject or theme. This will help search engines index your work more accurately and make it easier for people to find it online.

4. Create a title, desciption and tags

To make your digital art more discoverable, provide an engaging title and an accurate description for each piece you upload. Include keywords related to the themes or subjects present in your artwork as well as its style, medium, or technique.

Intermediate Guide to Designing NFTs

Tags are similar to keywords but provide a more straightforward way for viewers and search engines to find related content based on their interests. Ensure you include relevant tags that accurately describe your piece of art.

5. Consider copyright information

Adding copyright information to your digital art's metadata ensures that your work is appropriately credited and protected. Include the copyright symbol ©, the year of creation, and your name within the metadata to help secure your rights.

6. Add your contact information

Adding your contact information within the metadata of your digital art will assist potential clients or collaborators in getting in touch with you. Include essential details like your name, website, email address, and social media handles.

7. Export metadata correctly

When uploading digital art files online, ensure you maintain all carried metadata from previous steps during export.

Check if the platform or application you are using supports embedding metadata within image files like JPEGs or PNGs.

8. Test your uploads

Before making your digital art publicly available, test the upload process by viewing it on different devices and browsers. Make sure everything appears as intended and all accompanying information is displayed correctly.

By following these step-by-step instructions for formatting your digital art and adhering to metadata standards, you're setting yourself up for success in the online realm. Remember that proper organization and accurate information about your artwork can make a world of difference in increasing its visibility and impact.

Establishing Ownership of Your Digital Assets: A Step-by-Step Guide to Token Mapping

Token mapping is one process for doing just that. In this article, we'll provide a detailed step-by-step guide on how to establish ownership of your digital assets through token mapping.

Step 1: Understand the Concept of Token Mapping

Token mapping refers to the process of assigning a unique identifier or "digital fingerprint" to digital assets, linking them to their rightful owner's public address on the blockchain. This provides a secure, transparent, and tamper-proof record of ownership that can be easily verified.

Step 2: Choose a Blockchain Platform

Before you can map your digital assets, you need to decide on a platform that best meets your needs. You could choose from popular platforms like Ethereum, Binance Smart Chain, or Solana which support user-generated digital assets. Consider factors like transaction fees, security protocols, and community support when making your choice.

Step 3: Create Your Unique Public Address

To establish ownership of your digital assets on the chosen blockchain platform, create a unique public address - also known as a wallet address. This will serve as your digital identity on the network and will be linked to all your token mappings.

Step 4: Generate Your Digital Asset's Unique Identifier

Now it's time to create a unique identifier for each of your digital assets in order to tokenize them. In most cases, this will include information such as metadata and scarcity attributes which are vital in assessing the asset's value.

Step 5: Conduct the Token Mapping Process

With your public address and digital asset's unique identifier ready, proceed to link them in the blockchain's distributed ledger. This process involves creating a special transaction that embeds the unique identifier of your digital asset within your public address for record-keeping purposes.

Step 6: Verify Your Digital Asset's Ownership

Once the token mapping process is complete, you can verify the ownership of your assets by searching for their unique identifier on a blockchain explorer. This will display information about the token, including its current owner's public address and transaction history.

Step 7: Secure Your Private Keys

Never underestimate the importance of protecting your private keys – the cryptographic code that grants access to your digital assets. Store them securely, either using a hardware wallet or trusted software-based wallets with strong security features.

Step 8: Regularly Monitor Your Digital Assets

Keep an eye on your digital asset portfolio to ensure everything remains secure. Regularly check for updates or vulnerabilities on your chosen blockchain platform and stay informed about developments in the industry.

In conclusion, token mapping is an essential process for establishing and verifying ownership of digital assets. By following these steps, you can reinforce the security of your digital assets and ensure they remain accessible only by authorized parties. As you navigate the world of blockchain technology, be sure to stay informed about best practices to protect and benefit from your investments.

Demystifying Pricing and Token Economics: A Step-by-Step Guide to NFTs and Digital Assets

Many people are still puzzled by the seemingly complex world of pricing mechanisms and token economics. In this section, we'll demystify this topic by offering a detailed, step-by-step explanation of pricing and token economics with NFTs and digital assets.

Step 1: Understand the Basics of NFTs and Digital Assets

To get started, it's crucial to understand what NFTs and digital assets are. Non-fungible tokens (NFTs) are unique, indivisible tokens that represent ownership of a particular digital asset. Digital assets can include artwork, music, videos, virtual land, collectables, and much more.

Step 2: Explore the Role of Blockchain Technology

Blockchain technology is the backbone of digital asset transactions. Decentralized platforms such as Ethereum form the foundation for smooth transactions while providing transparency and security. Understanding how blockchain works will provide insights into NFTs' behavior and their associated values.

Step 3: Learn about Valuation Factors for Digital Assets

Valuing NFTs can be subjective since they involve unique items not directly comparable to others in the market. However, certain factors influence their value:

- Rarity: How scarce or common an item is in relation to its peers.

- Provenance: The origin or historical significance of the item.

- Utility: The usefulness or practical value it offers.

- Demand: How sought-after the item is among buyers.

Step 4: Appreciate the Concept of Tokenomics

Tokenomics (or token economics) refers to the study of how tokens operate within an ecosystem. This includes supply mechanisms, distribution strategies, and incentives for stakeholders. It's crucial to comprehend how an NFT project's tokenomics contributes to value creation.

Step 5: Analyze Different Pricing Models of NFTs

NFTs can have different pricing models depending on the nature of the project. Here are some common ones:

- Fixed price: Sellers set a non-negotiable price for their items.

- Auction: Buyers place bids, and the highest bid wins the auction.

- Yield farming: Users earn tokens in return for their participation in a platform that can be exchanged for NFTs.

- Royalty fees: A percentage of secondary sales gets paid to the original creators.

Step 6: Study Marketplaces and Platforms

Various platforms facilitate NFT transactions, but each one may differ in terms of fees, supported blockchain networks, and user interfaces. Some popular markets include OpenSea, Rarible, and SuperRare. These platforms will also help you understand prevalent pricing practices.

Step 7: Monitor NFT Trends and Market Sentiment

Digital asset values often reflect current trends, buzz, or market sentiment. Monitoring developments within the NFT ecosystem will offer valuable insights into potential price fluctuations.

In conclusion, understanding pricing and token economics is a vital part of navigating the world of digital assets and NFTs. By learning the fundamentals and staying informed about the latest trends, you'll be well-equipped to make educated decisions about buying or selling your unique tokens.

If you're looking to make a splash in this exciting market, it's crucial to know how to promote your NFTs effectively. In this comprehensive guide, we'll explore several key steps to successfully market and sell your NFTs.

1. Create high-quality, unique NFTs

The foundation of any successful NFT promotion campaign begins with the quality of your work. Make sure your NFTs are visually appealing, original, and showcase your creative talent. High-quality assets are more likely to attract potential buyers and stand out in the crowded marketplace.

2. Utilize social media platforms

Social media channels like Twitter, Instagram, and Facebook offer powerful ways to connect with potential buyers and showcase your NFTs. Share images, videos, or teasers of your work, engage with your audience through comments and direct messages, and make use of relevant hashtags to increase visibility.

Intermediate Guide to Designing NFTs

3. Build a dedicated website or landing page

Create a professional-looking website or landing page where potential buyers can learn more about your NFT collection. This will provide an easy way for them to view your portfolio, understand pricing structures (like auctions or fixed prices), and find links to where they can buy your tokens on various marketplaces.

4. Leverage NFT marketplaces

Upload your NFTs to popular marketplaces like OpenSea, Rarible, or SuperRare. These platforms have built-in audiences actively searching for new pieces to add to their collections. Create an eye-catching listing with a detailed description of each token's attributes to stand out from the competition.

5. Establish collaborations with influencers

Partner with influencers who have established followings in the crypto or art community. This could include artists who have already found success in the NFT space or reputable collectors who can vouch for your work's quality.

Collaborations with influencers can help you tap into their audience, amplifying the reach of your promotion efforts.

6. Foster a sense of community

Engage with potential buyers on online forums, NFT communities, and Discord channels. Build relationships with fellow creators and collectors to create a loyal following around your work. Sharing your journey as an emerging NFT artist within these forums can help you garner support, gain valuable feedback, and make crucial connections in the industry.

7. Offer limited editions or exclusives

Make your NFTs more appealing by offering limited editions or exclusive perks to early buyers. Scarcity can drive up the perceived value of your tokens, while exclusive perks (such as discounts on future releases or custom commissions) can encourage buyers to commit to purchasing.

8. Track success and optimize your strategy

Keep an eye on the success of your various promotional efforts. Analyze which tactics generate the most engagement or sales and adjust your marketing strategy accordingly over time.

Intermediate Guide to Designing NFTs

In conclusion, successfully promoting and selling NFTs requires a combination of compelling artwork, strategic marketing efforts, and active community engagement. By following these steps, you'll be well on your way to making a name for yourself in the booming NFT market.

Advanced topics

Cross-chain development and interoperability

As advanced NFT topics such as cross-chain development and interoperability are becoming increasingly relevant, it is crucial to understand these concepts for a deeper awareness of the potential of NFTs in today's market.

Cross-Chain Development: Bridging the Gap Between Blockchains

As decentralized platforms gain popularity, multiple blockchain networks with unique strengths and features have arisen. However, one limiting factor remains: these blockchains often function as isolated ecosystems. This is where cross-chain development comes into play. Cross-chain development aims to create a technology that allows for seamless interaction and collaboration between different blockchain networks.

In the NFT space, this allows users to move their digital assets and tokens across various blockchains without any barriers. For instance, an artist could mint an NFT on Ethereum but later decide to transfer it to another platform like Binance Smart Chain or Polkadot to take advantage of lower fees or different functionalities.

Interoperability: The Path Towards Unified Operations

Interoperability refers to the ability of different systems or platforms to work together harmoniously. In the context of blockchain and NFTs, this implies that tokens created on one blockchain can be effortlessly utilized on another.

Various initiatives have surfaced intending to solve interoperability challenges:

1. Inter-Blockchain Communication (IBC): IBC is a protocol that facilitates communication between blockchains while maintaining each network's security properties. This approach allows NFTs issued on one platform to be used on others through the creation of "contexts" standardizing token information.

2. Wrapped Tokens: Wrapped tokens are significantly contributing to NFT interoperability by enabling assets from one blockchain network (e.g.,

Bitcoin) to be represented on another (e.g., Ethereum). The wrapping process involves locking an original token and then minting a new token on the target blockchain with the same value.

3. Oracle Networks: Oracle networks act as intermediaries between blockchains, providing data and information essential for cross-chain communication. They enable NFT platforms to maintain consistency across blockchains by verifying the authenticity and state of digital assets during cross-chain transfers.

The Future of Cross-Chain NFTs

As NFTs continue to gain traction globally, the need for cross-chain development and interoperability becomes increasingly more critical. By enabling seamless interaction between different blockchains, users will enjoy greater flexibility, improved utility, and increased value from their digital assets. In turn, this will foster widespread adoption and bring a robust ecosystem that embraces the limitless potential of NFTs.

In conclusion, understanding advanced NFT topics like cross-chain development and interoperability are crucial in today's rapidly evolving blockchain landscape. Focusing on bridging the gap between various blockchain networks is essential not only for greater utility but also for increased mass adoption of NFTs.

As these technologies continue to evolve, we can expect a future where users interact freely with their digital assets regardless of their originating blockchain platform.

Developing NFTs for Multiple Blockchain Platforms: A Comprehensive Guide

How can you create NFTs that can exist on multiple blockchain platforms? In this comprehensive guide, we'll explore the process of developing NFTs for diverse blockchain ecosystems.

1. Understand the Basics of NFTs

Before diving into multi-platform NFT development, it's crucial to comprehend the fundamentals of non-fungible tokens. Unlike other cryptocurrencies like Bitcoin or Ethereum, NFTs are not interchangeable due to their distinctive attributes. They often represent digital art pieces, virtual goods, or other one-of-a-kind assets and are typically based on Ethereum's ERC-721 or ERC-1155 token standards.

2. Choose Your Blockchain Platforms

As NFT popularity grows, multiple blockchain platforms are emerging as viable alternatives to Ethereum – each offering different benefits and

Intermediate Guide to Designing NFTs

drawbacks. Some commonly considered options include Binance Smart Chain (BSC), Flow, and Tezos. Assess your target audience and specific requirements before deciding which blockchains to focus on. You may want to consider transaction fees, network speed, and existing marketplaces when making your choice.

3. Develop Cross-Chain Compatibility

To make NFTs compatible with multiple blockchains, you need to employ a cross-chain development approach. This involves creating separate smart contracts for each platform while ensuring they can communicate with one another seamlessly through a shared standard.

One notable solution is adopting a multi-token framework like the ERC-998 standard that allows for composing both fungible (ERC-20) and non-fungible tokens into a single contract. This enables you to create an NFT that can be transferred across different blockchains while maintaining its identity.

4. Utilize Interoperable NFT Marketplaces

Once your NFTs are compatible with multiple blockchains, consider leveraging interoperable marketplaces to ease the process of buying, selling, and trading these tokens.

Platforms like Rarible and OpenSea allow users to list, discover, and transact NFTs across several networks, providing a smooth experience for your audience.

5. Optimize Your NFT Metadata

To enhance the SEO-friendliness of your NFT listings, ensure you provide accurate and descriptive metadata associated with each token. This includes the token name, description, tags, and creator information. Optimized metadata not only helps buyers efficiently find your NFTs in marketplaces but also improves their visibility on search engines.

6. Market and Promote Your Multi-Platform NFTs

Finally, engage in active marketing efforts to promote your cross-platform NFTs across social media channels, online communities focused on digital art and collectibles, and relevant industry events. Regularly share updates on new releases or collaborations, providing insight into the creative process and showcasing the unique benefits of your multi-platform approach.

In conclusion, developing NFTs for multiple blockchain platforms requires a deep understanding of non-fungible tokens and cross-chain compatibility techniques.

Intermediate Guide to Designing NFTs

By carefully selecting the right networks and optimizing your assets for multiple environments, you can capture a more significant share of the booming NFT market while providing unique value to collectors across diverse ecosystems.

NFT Royalties and Secondary Sales: A Comprehensive Guide

In this section, we'll dive deep into NFT royalties and secondary sales, explaining how they work and why they're so important for artists in today's rapidly evolving digital landscape.

Understanding NFT Royalties

Royalties refer to the ongoing earnings an artist receives from their work even after it's been sold. In the physical art world, royalties typically come from licensing agreements or reproduction rights. However, with NFTs, royalties function differently.

When minting an NFT, artists can set a specific royalty percentage to be received every time their work is resold on a secondary market. Most platforms that support NFT minting allow creators to set customizable royalty rates between 0% to 100%. Every time the NFT is sold thereafter, a portion of the sale proceeds goes directly to the original creator as a royalty.

Intermediate Guide to Designing NFTs

The Power of Secondary Sales

Secondary sales are essential to understanding the potential earnings from NFT royalties. Once an artist sells their NFT on a primary marketplace (e.g., OpenSea or Rarible), it may change hands multiple times among collectors through secondary markets.

Secondary markets provide a platform for buyers and sellers to trade previously owned NFTs. With every resale transaction, the original creator receives their set royalty percentage from the sale price. This ensures that as long as there's demand for their work in the market, artists continue to generate passive income.

The Benefits of NFT Royalties and Secondary Sales

There are several advantages to incorporating royalties into your NFT strategy:

1. Sustainable Income: By receiving a percentage of every resale transaction, creators can enjoy a sustainable income source that's not limited to initial sales. This creates a more balanced revenue stream and helps support artists even when they're not actively minting new NFTs.

2. Valuation Boost: NFTs with built-in royalties encourage collectors to

invest in them, as part of the value lies in ongoing earnings. If an artist's work gains popularity, the potential for increased royalties boosts the overall value of the NFT.

3. Long-term Incentives: Since artists continue benefiting from resales, they have an incentive to create high-quality, unique work that retains its value over time. This fosters a healthier market and encourages long-term growth for both artists and collectors.

Final Thoughts

NFT royalties and secondary sales offer incredible opportunities for creators and collectors alike, empowering them to benefit from ongoing demand for their digital creations. By understanding how these processes work and incorporating royalty percentages into your NFT strategy, you can maximize your earnings potential and support a more sustainable creative ecosystem in the exciting world of digital art.

Exploring the Future of Entertainment: NFT Gaming and Virtual Worlds

Over the past few years, the gaming industry has been transformed by the rapid development of cutting-edge technologies. One such groundbreaking innovation is the rise of Non-Fungible Tokens (NFTs), which have started to revolutionize virtual worlds and online gaming. In the next few paragraphs, we dive into a detailed explanation of NFT gaming and virtual worlds, exploring how they are reshaping the future of digital entertainment.

Defining NFTs and Their Role in Gaming

NFTs are unique digital assets that cannot be exchanged at a one-to-one ratio like cryptocurrencies (e.g., Bitcoin). Their uniqueness, scarcity, and ability to prove ownership make them valuable collectables within virtual environments. By utilizing blockchain technology, NFTs provide proof of ownership, provenance, and secure transferability.

In the gaming context, NFTs enable gamers to own in-game assets like skins, weapons, or virtual land. These tokenized assets can be bought, sold, or traded on various platforms, empowering players with true ownership and monetization opportunities.

The Emergence of Virtual Worlds

Virtual worlds have existed for decades in various forms; however, the concept has evolved significantly with advancements in technology. Today's virtual worlds provide immersive experiences backed by powerful gaming engines, vivid graphics, and an increasing degree of interactivity among users.

These digital realms mimic the real world in many aspects – persistent environments that evolve with time, economies where users can buy or sell goods/services and social interactions that forge human connections. Additionally, innovations like NFTs offer users more freedom to express themselves artistically or create new revenue streams via digital asset ownership.

Blurring Boundaries: NFT Gaming Meets Virtual Worlds

The intersection between NFT gaming and virtual worlds is already making strides. Games like Decentraland and The Sandbox provide players with fully immersive metaverses where NFTs play a crucial role. Users can purchase, construct, customize and monetize virtual land using NFTs, thereby granting them more agency over their online experience.

Moreover, in-game assets are not restricted to a single game or platform. These mutable assets can be moved, integrated or combined across different games utilizing interoperable NFT standards. This cross-platform compatibility opens the door to unique gaming experiences and value appreciation for game developers and gamers alike.

The Road Ahead

The fusion of NFT gaming and virtual worlds promises to radically expand the landscape of digital entertainment.

As more developers continue to explore this nascent industry's potential, we can anticipate seeing even more elaborate and sophisticated virtual universes emerge.

From digital art galleries and smart-contracts-enabled marketplaces to interactive music festivals, NFT gaming and virtual worlds will undoubtedly continue pushing the boundaries of innovation. By fostering enhanced ownership, creativity, and monetization opportunities, NFTs will play an instrumental role in shaping the future of online gaming experiences.

Case studies and success stories

Notable NFT projects, artists, and creators

Let's now explore notable NFT projects and the talented artists and creators behind them. So let's dive in!

1. CryptoPunks - The Pioneers of NFTs

Launched in 2017 by software developers Matt Hall and John Watkinson, CryptoPunks was one of the first NFT projects that gained widespread attention. A collection of 10,000 unique pixel-art characters, CryptoPunks paved the way for digital art ownership through blockchain technology.

Each character could be bought and sold using Ethereum cryptocurrency — today some of these iconic characters sell for millions of dollars.

2. Beeple - From Digital Art Contender to Headliner

Mike Winkelmann, better known as Beeple, has been producing digital art for over a decade. But it was his NFT masterpiece "Everydays: The First 5000 Days" that thrust him into the limelight. This digital collage showcases 5,000 pieces of his work crafted daily between 2007 and 2021. Sold at Christie's auction house for a shocking $69 million, Beeple's work ranks as one of the most expensive pieces sold among living artists.

3. NBA Top Shot - A Sports Fan's Fantasy Come True

NBA Top Shot is a one-of-a-kind platform where enthusiasts can own officially licensed NBA-featured video moments referred to as "Moments." Developed by Dapper Labs in partnership with the NBA and Players Association, it allows fans to build their unique collection of basketball highlights. With Moment prices ranging from just a few dollars to hundreds of thousands, NBA Top Shot has quickly become an NFT sensation—from die-hard fans to casual followers.

4. Sorare - The Fantasy Football Playground

Sorare is an NFT-powered fantasy football game allowing participants to create and manage their soccer teams using digital player cards. These officially licensed cards come in different scarcity levels, impacting their price and performance. The platform has attracted over 130 licensed clubs, including global names like Paris Saint-Germain and Juventus, creating a bustling marketplace for NFT soccer cards.

5. Async Art - Exploring Programmable Art

Async Art is an innovative NFT platform that allows artists to create flexible "programmable" artworks that change over time or based on external factors, such as market fluctuations or user inputs. Spanning a wide range of genres and styles, Async's mutable art pieces give collectors and viewers an engaging, interactive experience taking digital art to new heights.

These examples merely scratch the surface of the burgeoning world of NFTs. The success stories of CryptoPunks, Beeple, NBA Top Shot, Sorare, and Async Art are just the start as technology continues to break boundaries in the artistic realm. Whether you're an artist, investor or simply a curious observer, there's no denying that NFTs offer unprecedented opportunities for the creative world at large.

The Soaring Success of NFT Launches: Lessons Learned from the Past

The Non-Fungible Token (NFT) market has exploded in recent years, with numerous successful launches proving the potential of this innovative technology. Entrepreneurs, artists, and collectors are flocking to tap into the lucrative world of NFTs, and there is much to learn from these pioneering projects. As we delve into the lessons learned from successful NFT launches in the past, let's identify some key ingredients for driving success in this ever-evolving landscape.

1. Create a Unique and Intriguing Concept

Standing out in a crowded market is critical to any NFT launch. One key strategy adopted by successful projects is to offer an original and attention-grabbing concept. For example, CryptoPunks redefined the NFT art world by presenting characters with unique traits, creating value through scarcity and uniqueness. When planning your NFT project, consider not only what sets your idea apart but also how it can capture an audience's imagination.

2. Establish a Strong Community Base

It's no secret that community plays a vital role in the success of any NFT launch. Many successful projects have fostered communities through social media platforms and dedicated forums where followers can engage with one another, share news, and get involved in the project's development. This sense of belonging not only helps spread awareness about your project but also establishes a sense of trust and loyalty among potential buyers.

3. Leverage Influencers and Collaborations

Influencer marketing has proved effective for many NFT launches. By collaborating with well-known figures or partnering with established brands within your niche, you can tap into an existing audience eager to explore your project. For instance, Bored Ape Yacht Club became a sensation partly because of its endorsements from high-profile individuals like NBA star Stephen Curry and rapper Post Malone.

4. Prioritize Transparency & Fair Distribution

A common issue faced by the NFT market is the fear of scams and fraud. Addressing this concern through transparency in your project's development and a fair distribution model is essential for long-term success. Many notable NFT projects have secured trust by openly communicating their team members, goals, and roadmap as well as ensuring a level playing field for buyers during launch events.

5. Plan Cross-Platform Integration and Utility

One of the exciting aspects of NFTs is their ability to interact with different platforms, such as virtual reality applications, games, or other digital art experiences. By offering cross-platform integration opportunities or utilities for your NFT — like exclusive access to content or special rewards for owners — you can increase its value and appeal.

In conclusion, successful NFT launches in the past have showcased pioneering concepts, fostered strong communities, leveraged influencers, prioritized transparency, and embraced cross-platform integration. By applying these learnings to your own NFT journey, you too can unlock tremendous potential in this dynamic and innovative space

Conclusion and future outlook

Potential uses of NFTs beyond digital art and collectibles

Predictions for the evolution of the NFT market and technology

The Future Outlook for NFTs: Beyond Digital Art and Collectibles

The NFT market is not limited to just these sectors.

With new and innovative uses for NFTs cropping up every day, let's finish up by diving into the potential applications of NFTs beyond digital art and collectables while predicting how the market and technology might evolve in the future.

Potential Uses of NFTs Beyond Digital Art and Collectibles

1. Gaming and Virtual Worlds: NFTs have already found a place in gaming by representing unique, tradeable in-game assets such as weapons, vehicles, or characters. In virtual worlds such as Decentraland or The Sandbox, players can also own virtual land as NFTs, which can be developed or resold.

2. Intellectual Property: From music to film, creators can tokenize their digital content as NFTs and sell limited editions directly to consumers. This not only offers a new revenue stream for artists but also combats piracy by establishing a clear chain of ownership.

3. Physical Assets: Tokenizing real-world assets like property, luxury goods, or even event tickets as NFTs can provide improved security and transferability of ownership. This enables easier transactions while reducing fraud in the process.

4. Identity Verification: By creating unique digital identities as NFTs, individuals can easily prove their identity across various platforms without sharing sensitive personal information.

Predictions for the Evolution of the NFT Market and Technology

1. Improved Interoperability and Scalability: As blockchain networks continue to evolve, more advanced standards for creating and trading NFTs will likely emerge. This could result in better interoperability between different blockchains and decrease transaction costs while allowing more people to access the market.

2. Enhanced Security Measures: As the value of NFTs increases, so does the need for robust security measures. We can expect to see the development of new security protocols and technologies to protect both creators and collectors in the NFT marketplace.

3. Better Curation and Discovery: As the number of NFTs available continues to grow, more sophisticated curation methods and discovery platforms will likely be developed to help users find high-quality content that matches their interests.

4. Mainstream Adoption: As the utility of NFTs grows beyond art and collectables, we can expect a broader segment of the population to

embrace this novel technology. Major brands and traditional industries will likely start experimenting with NFTs for a variety of applications, further integrating them into mainstream culture.

In conclusion, the future outlook for NFTs is bright as they continue to disrupt various industries beyond digital art and collectables. With improved technology, increased security features, and mainstream adoption just around the corner, the potential for NFTs is only limited by our imagination. So keep an eye on this burgeoning market – it might just change the way we think about ownership, trade, and value in the digital age.

What next?   **COMING SOON**   Look out for the next book on Amazon.com

Journey into the Metaverse: A New Digital Frontier

Course Outline:

I. Introduction

    A. Definition of the metaverse

    B. The concept's origin and evolution

    C. How the metaverse will reshape our world

Intermediate Guide to Designing NFTs

II. History of Virtual Worlds and the Emergence of the Metaverse

    A. Early virtual worlds and online gaming

    B. The rise of social networks and digital identity

    C. The role of augmented reality and virtual reality technologies

III. Key Components of the Metaverse

    A. Persistent virtual landscapes

    B. Interoperability between platforms

    C. Digital assets and tokenization of economies

    D. Digital avatars and volumetric capture

IV. Influential Companies Shaping the Metaverse

    A. Meta (formerly Facebook)

    B. Epic Games (creator of Unreal Engine and Fortnite)

    C. Microsoft and its HoloLens technology

    D. Google Earth VR, ARCore, and other Google initiatives

    E. Emerging startups in the space

V. Imagination Meets Reality: Use Cases for the Metaverse

    A. Gaming and immersive entertainment

B. Collaboration and remote workspaces

C.Floor_GF1.Intro0 Marketing, advertising, and brand experiences

D.Social interactions, connecting people across boundaries

VI.Educational Implications of the Metaverse

A.Transformation in teaching

B.Virtual classrooms

C.Opportunities for immersive learning

VII.Technological Innovations Driving the Metaverse's Growth

A.Blockchain technology and decentralized finance (DeFi)

B.Advancements in VR/AR hardware

C.Artificial intelligence (AI)

VIII.Challenges & Ethical Considerations within the Metaverse

A.Digital divide

B.Security, privacy, and data ownership

C.Social impact and mental health concerns

IX.Futuristic Predictions: The Metaverse in 10 Years

A. Advancement in key metaverse technologies

Intermediate Guide to Designing NFTs

B. Changes in everyday life due to the metaverse's integration

C. Societal impacts and new norms within the metaverse

X.Conclusion

A.Reflection on the potential of the metaverse

B.Closing thoughts on embracing this digital frontier

End

Intermediate Guide to Designing NFTs